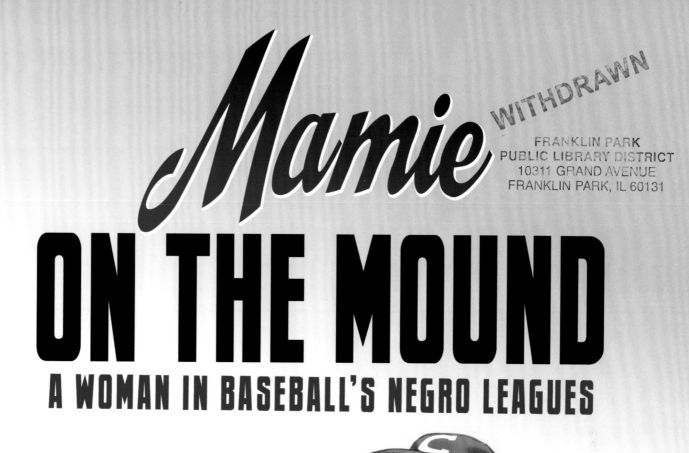

Mamie
ON THE MOUND
A WOMAN IN BASEBALL'S NEGRO LEAGUES

by Leah Henderson
illustrated by George Doutsiopoulos

CAPSTONE EDITIONS
a capstone imprint

Mamie Johnson stepped on the mound to pitch in one of her first Negro League games. She knew she was ready. She was the first female pitcher in professional baseball. Even if others doubted a woman could pitch to the fellas, she didn't.

"How do you expect to strike anyone out and you're not as big as a peanut?" an opposing batter yelled.

Only 5 feet 4 inches tall and
barely 120 pounds, Mamie smirked.
STRIKE ONE...
STRIKE TWO...
STRIKE THREE...
The batter found himself
back on the bench quickly, but the
name *Peanut* stuck. And on that
day in 1953, another individual
realized not to underestimate
Mamie "Peanut" Johnson.

Mamie Johnson had been about six years old when her uncle Leo, who was close in age, started teaching her all he knew about baseball. Mamie took to the sport right away, only complaining to her grandma whenever the boys wouldn't let her play. Mamie didn't want to watch from the bleachers with the other girls in their Sunday best and white gloves. She wanted to be on the mound, her pitcher's mitt snug around her fingers.

Girls at that time weren't often encouraged to be athletes, but Mamie's family supported her love of the game. They always told her to follow her heart.

Mamie grew up running over bases made of broken flowerpots and pie plates, and sliding to reach home, a lid from a five-gallon can of King Cane syrup. Swinging a tree limb for a bat, she knocked homemade balls of stone wrapped with twine and masking tape. That's how Mamie got her start in baseball—playing with the boys in Ridgeway, South Carolina, on her family's 80-acre farm.

When Mamie was about ten, her grandmother passed away, and Mamie moved from the rural South to the North. While her mother worked hard to buy a house for the family in Washington, D.C., Mamie was sent to live with her aunt and uncle in Long Branch, New Jersey. Although her school was no longer filled with black faces, Mamie was okay. She had little trouble at her previously all-white school, because she knew, as she later told it, "Hey, I'm just as smart as you."

Mamie's confidence walked step for step with her ability to play baseball. She knew she was as good as—if not better than—any opponent she encountered. She just needed to be given the chance to prove it.

She knew people took one look at her and doubted her ability. But that was all right with Mamie.

Their doubts only strengthened her secret weapon.

Over and over again, she proved them wrong with her strong right arm.

In Long Branch, Mamie tried playing softball with the girls, but never took to it. Instead she played catch with Leo. But she wanted more.

After school one day, she took a shortcut home and came across a group of boys playing ball in a sandlot. They were on a Police Athletic League team. Mamie wanted to join. Remembering the words of her grandma—*the good Lord helps those who help themselves*—Mamie marched into the police station and asked for the opportunity to try out.

Even though the Long Branch Police Athletic League was an all-white, all-boys league, the coach of the team gave Mamie the chance to try. Some of the boys may have snickered or laughed at first, but when she stepped up on the mound and let the ball fly from her strong right arm, they realized she was there to play. During her time on the team, she helped her teammates win two division championships.

The more Mamie played baseball, the better she got and the more she wanted to play. She realized, however, that she already had two strikes against her:

She was a girl.

She was black.

"The black boys not even playin' so I know I'm not gonna make it," she huffed. For the first time, her dream of being a professional baseball player began to dim.

Then, on April 15, 1947, all that changed. Jackie Robinson, a black man, joined Major League Baseball. Could Mamie actually have only one strike against her?

Robinson played first base for the Brooklyn Dodgers. If Jackie could break the color line and become Major League Baseball's first black player, Mamie could break the gender line.

"You can do this too," she told herself. Once again, her dream brightened.

At age 11, Mamie moved to Washington, D.C., to live with her mother. After graduating from high school, she continued playing sandlot baseball on local semipro men's teams. Then one day her teammate and friend Rita Jones told Mamie the All-American Girls Professional Baseball League was having tryouts near them.

"We can do this," they told each other, and they took a bus across the bridge to Alexandria, Virginia.

Ready to prove they deserved spots, they hopped off the bus and raced to the ball field to join hundreds of other girls and women eager to try out. Mamie and Rita quickly realized, however, that they weren't getting past the foul lines.

A field full of white players stared at them. Even though Mamie and Rita had their gloves and looked ready to play like everyone else, it didn't matter.

"I guess we better go," Mamie said, staring back. "I don't think we're wanted here."

Rita agreed, and they left.

Even with Jackie Robinson breaking the color barrier in Major League Baseball a few years before, the All-American Girls Professional Baseball League wasn't ready to give black women the opportunity to try.

All was still not equal.

"They think I'm not as good," Mamie said. She shook the thought away, knowing it wasn't true. She was as good as any player on that team.

Prejudice wasn't going to stop her from playing the game she loved. In fact, being refused that chance opened up an even greater opportunity to Mamie.

"You wanna play pro baseball?" Bish Tyson, a former Negro League player, called to her one day.

Mamie gave a chuckle like he'd asked if the sky was above her. "Yeah," she answered.

"Go to the Dunbar Hotel tomorrow in your uniform and ask for Mr. Bunny Downs," he said.

Mamie didn't think twice or ask any questions. After a brief meeting at the hotel the next day, she tried out on a nearby field. She wasn't scared. She was ready. She'd been practicing her entire life.

Now she had the chance to prove she belonged.

The following day, she quit her job at a local ice cream shop and slipped away from her mother and her new family, a husband and baby son.

Mamie was headstrong, and no one, not even her baby boy, was going to stop her. She was joining the Indianapolis Clowns for two months of "bus baseball."

Going from town to town on a bus filled with men, playing doubleheaders and tripleheaders against any team willing to play them wasn't always the easiest, but Mamie didn't care. At age nineteen, her dream was coming true.

She was playing pro baseball.

The only other female player on the Indianapolis Clowns, a second baseman named Toni Stone, had joined the team a year before. The women had signed to the Negro Leagues at a time when many of its best players—Willie Mays, Ernie Banks, Larry Doby, Hank Aaron, Satchel Paige, and others— were leaving for the brighter lights of the Major Leagues.

Unfortunately, fans and sportswriters followed the stars, making it harder for black teams to survive. Empty seats in stadiums meant empty wallets for team owners and players.

Like the three circus clowns who traveled with the team, Mamie and Toni knew they were hired to draw curious fans. But the women didn't do any clowning.

Toni was ready to catch and hit.

Mamie was ready to throw—a fastball, circle change, slider, screwball, or curveball.

They weren't passing up their opportunity.

"I'm here to play ball. I ain't here to do nothin' else but play ball," Mamie said. "And I'm gonna show you I can play just as good as you."

At first the male players looked at Mamie like she was too small. They grumbled about sharing the field with her, Toni, and later Connie Morgan, a second baseman who played with the Clowns after Toni was traded. But like every other time, Mamie was ready to prove she belonged. Some of the players were slow to understand that the women were part of the team now. Mr. Downs, the Clowns' manager, set the players straight.

"If y'all think you can't handle that," he said, pointing to the girls, "we'll take you down to the bus station tomorrow. We'll get someone who can go along with the program."

The men may have laughed, at first, but they knew
Mr. Downs was serious.

"These girls are putting money in your pocket," Mr. Downs
said. "Think about that. . . . And the girls can play, so treat the
girls right. Treat 'em like they're one of you. That's all I ask you
to do."

That is exactly what the men did as soon as Mamie's fastball whizzed over home plate. After she won their first game together, she had little trouble from her teammates. They became twenty-six brothers on the road with her.

Life with the Clowns wasn't just about hitting balls and striking players out—or cracking jokes and playing cards on the bus. In some places, it was about whites-only water fountains, whites-only service at restaurants, and whites-only hotels. It was about 10 p.m. curfews for black men, closed locker rooms, closed concession stands, and closed bathrooms for black players and black fans. It meant being on the bus for three or four days in sweaty uniforms. Even if white people came to see them play or even competed against them, Mamie and her teammates weren't always welcome to eat or sleep in their towns in the segregated South of the Jim Crow era.

The buses took the players far and wide. During Mamie's first year with the Clowns, they traveled across the country and into Canada. Living out of a suitcase wasn't always comfortable, but in some towns, local black families would take Mamie, Toni, and Connie in. They'd get a warm meal and a bed for the night, while the male players were left to sleep in dingy hotels or under the stars.

Chicago

Indianapolis

Cincinnati

Nashville

Little Rock

But if asked, Mamie never let the hard times bother her too much. She would say, "Don't emphasize the hardness of it," because she and the other players were doing what they wanted to do—playing the game they loved. She and her teammates filled the stands at Comiskey Park and Yankee Stadium, even when white ball clubs couldn't.

Watched by cheering fans, Peanut often pitched seven, eight, or nine innings and struck out many of her opponents. Even though baseball was all she ever wanted to do, her dream did have a limit. The Major Leagues weren't ready to give her or any other woman a chance to play. So during the off-season, Mamie studied engineering and nursing at New York University and later in North Carolina. For her, there were dreams beyond baseball.

Mamie loved nothing more than winding up, firing away from the mound, and striking out batters. She built an impressive 33-8 record during her three seasons with the Clowns. She may have been small, but she had a strong right arm and used it to follow her heart, becoming the first female pitcher in professional baseball history. When Mamie stepped off the mound in 1955 to return to her family, she never strayed far from baseball—the game she would always love.

"I was a ballplayer. This is what I was and this is the way I want to be known, a ballplayer."

Mamie "Peanut" Johnson
1935–2017

AFTERWORD

After Mamie left the sport, she received a nursing degree from North Carolina A&T. Then she went home to Washington, D.C., to raise her young son. There, she was a licensed practical nurse for nearly thirty years.

During President Bill Clinton's time in office, he and First Lady Hillary Clinton honored Mamie at the White House as a Female Baseball Legend. In 2013, President Barack Obama also recognized her and other Negro League players for their accomplishments. Mamie attended various functions around the country where she could reminisce about what she called "the three best years of my life."

Long after her professional days, Mamie continued playing sandlot baseball, using the curveball that Negro League All-Star and Major League pitcher Satchel Paige helped her perfect. One of her greatest joys after leaving the game was coaching whenever she could. She even started the Mamie Johnson Little League in 2015. Underestimating no one, she encouraged all her players to follow their heart. Mamie Johnson helped clear the plate for pitchers such as Eri Yoshida, Tiffany Brooks, Ila Borders, and Mo'ne Davis and will always be remembered just as she wanted to be—as a ballplayer.

Leah Henderson was one of only two girls on a highly competitive "all-boys" traveling soccer team when she was young, so Mamie's desire to play ball echoed her own. Leah is the author of several books for young readers, including Children's Africana Book Awards notable, *One Shadow on the Wall*. She is a mentor and avid traveler, and her volunteer work has roots in West Africa. Leah holds an MFA in writing and is on faculty in Spalding University's MFA program. She currently calls Washington, D.C., home.

George Doutsiopoulos graduated from the School of Economics of the Aristotle University of Thessaloniki in Greece in 2005, but he decided to pursue a career in illustration, his true passion. In 2006, he won a prestigious comic competition and received a three-year full scholarship to AKTO Applied Arts College in Athens, Greece. He specializes in illustrations for books, board games, online games, and advertising. In addition, George teaches drawing, sketching, and illustration to children and adults.

Thank you to our adviser for his expertise, research, and advice:
Raymond Doswell, Ed.D., Vice President of Curatorial Services at Negro Leagues Baseball Museum in Kansas City, Missouri

Mamie on the Mound is published by
Capstone Editions, a Capstone imprint
1710 Roe Crest Drive, North Mankato, Minnesota 56003
www.capstonepub.com

J-B
JOHNSON
475-3631

Cataloging-in-Publication Data is available on the Library of Congress website.
ISBN: 978-1-68446-023-6 (library binding)
ISBN: 978-1-68446-024-3 (eBook PDF)

Summary: Rejected by the all-white All-American Girls Professional Baseball League, Mamie "Peanut" Johnson was happily signed by the Indianapolis Clowns in the Negro Leagues in 1953, and she became the only professional female pitcher to play on a men's team. During the three years she played with the team, her record was an impressive 33-8.

Photo credits: Negro League Baseball Museum, Inc.

Designed by: Ted Williams

Source Notes

"How do you . . . ?" Donna Britt, "Following Her Heart to Pitcher's Mound," *Washington Post,* September 10, 1999, https://www.washingtonpost.com/archive/local/1999/09/10/following-her-heart-to-pitchers-mound/88af4be8-0a07-400e-a899-b548c03198eb/?utm_term=.dd6940f9400c Accessed June 5, 2019.

"Hey, I'm just . . ." National Visionary Leadership Project, MPJ: Growing Up in Ridgeway, South Carolina, http://www.visionaryproject.org/johnsonmamie/ Accessed June 5, 2019.

"The black boys . . ." Ibid.

"You can do . . ." Ibid.

"We can do this." Ibid.

"I guess we better go . . ." Alan Schwarz. "Breaking Gender Barriers in the Negro Leagues," *The New York Times,* June 12, 2010, https://www.nytimes.com/2010/06/13/sports/baseball/13pitcher.html Accessed June 5, 2019.

"They think I'm . . ." Jean Hastings Ardell, "Mamie 'Peanut' Johnson: The Last Female Voice of the Negro Leagues." *Out of the Shadows: African American Baseball from the Cuban Giants to Jackie Robinson,* edited by Bill Kirwin, Lincoln: University of Nebraska Press, 2005, pp. 116-126.

"You wanna play pro baseball? . . ." National Visionary Leadership Project.

"I'm here to play ball. I ain't here to do nothin' else but play ball . . ." Ibid.

"If y'all think you can't handle that . . ." Brent Kelly. *Negro Leagues Revisited: Conversations with 66 More Baseball Heroes.* Jefferson: McFarland & Co, 2000.

"Don't emphasize . . ." *Out of the Shadows: African American Baseball from the Cuban Giants to Jackie Robinson.*

Select Bibliography

Ardell, Jean Hastings. "Mamie 'Peanut' Johnson: The Last Female Voice of the Negro Leagues." *Out of the Shadows: African American Baseball from the Cuban Giants to Jackie Robinson,* edited by Bill Kirwin, Lincoln: University of Nebraska Press, 2005, pp. 116-126.

Corey, Mary E., and Mark Harnischfeger. *Before Jackie: The Negro Leagues, Civil Rights and the American Dream.* Ithaca: Paramount Books, 2014.

Kelley, Brent. *Negro Leagues Revisited: Conversations with 66 More Baseball Heroes.* Jefferson: McFarland & Co, 2000.

Katz, Brigit. "Remembering Mamie 'Peanut' Johnson, the First Woman to Take the Mound as a Major-League Pitcher," *The Smithsonian.com,* December 26, 2017. https://www.smithsonianmag.com/smart-news/mamie-peanut-johnson-first-female-pitcher-negro-leagues-has-died-82-180967642/ Accessed June 5, 2019.

"Mamie 'Peanut' Johnson: Oral History Biography: National Visionary Oral History Archive," *National Visionary Leadership Project: African American History,* http://www.visionaryproject.org/johnsonmamie/ Accessed June 5, 2019.

Schwarz, Alan. "Breaking Gender Barriers in the Negro Leagues," *The New York Times,* June 12, 2010. https://www.nytimes.com/2010/06/13/sports/baseball/13pitcher.html Accessed June 5, 2019.

Silverman, Dan. "No League of Their Own: Barred from All-White Leagues, Three Women Found a Place to Play," *MLB.com,* http://mlb.mlb.com/mlb/history/mlb_negro_leagues_story.jsp?story=women Accessed June 5, 2019.

Printed in China.
2493

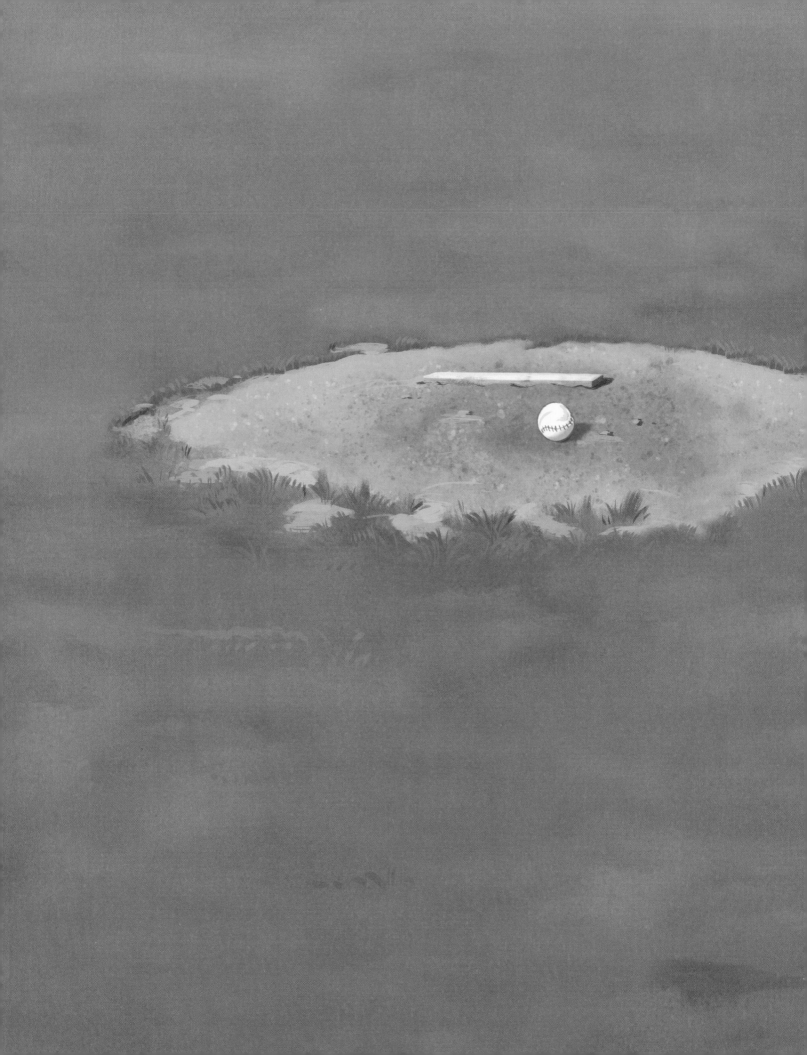